MACMILLAN READERS

BEGINNER LEVEL

ANNE COLLINS

Princess Diana

W0099750

MACMILLAN

BEGINNER LEVEL

Founding Editor: John Milne

The Macmillan Readers provide a choice of enjoyable reading materials for learners of English. The series is published at six levels – Starter, Beginner, Elementary, Pre-intermediate, Intermediate and Upper.

Level Control

Information, structure and vocabulary are controlled to suit the students' ability at each level.

The number of words at each level:

Starter	about 300 basic words
Beginner	about 600 basic words
Elementary	about 1100 basic words
Pre-intermediate	about 1400 basic words
Intermediate	about 1600 basic words
Upper	about 2200 basic words

Answer Keys

An Answer Key for the *Exercises* section can be found at www.macmillanenglish.com/readers

Audio Download

There is an audio download available for this title.
Visit www.macmillanenglish.com/readers for more information.

Contents

Introduction   4

1 The Early Years   4
2 The Prince   9
3 The Fairy Story Begins   13
4 'We Want Di!'   19
5 The Problems Begin   22
6 Unhappy Times   26
7 A Terrible Year   29
8 Princess Alone   31
9 The Road to Divorce   35
10 Starting a New Life   38
11 New Love   41
12 The Last Summer   43
13 The People's Princess   49
14 After Diana's Death   52

Exercises   55
Diana's Charities   63

Introduction

Princess Diana was a very famous British woman. In August 1997 Diana was on holiday in the Mediterranean with her new man, Dodi Al Fayed. There were holiday photographs of them in the newspapers. Diana looked happy. Then, just a few days later, she was dead. She died suddenly on the 31st of August in a car accident in Paris.

There are many books about Diana's life. We often see her photograph and hear her name. She was beautiful and famous. She was a modern Princess and a loving mother. She wanted to help people. But her life was not always happy. This is Diana's story.

1

The Early Years

Diana's parents were Frances and Johnnie Spencer, the Viscount Althorp. Johnnie was from a very old and important English family, the Spencer family. George Washington, Humphrey Bogart and Rudolph Valentino were connected to this family. Frances was beautiful but she was also a very strong woman. She fell in love with Johnnie Althorp when she was only seventeen years old. Johnnie Althorp was tall and handsome, and Frances wanted to marry him. Johnnie went to Eton – one of the most famous private schools in England – and then he was an officer in the army. Later he left the army and studied farming.

Frances and Johnnie married on the 1st of June 1954 at St Margaret's Church, Westminster, in London. A thousand people were at the wedding. The Queen, the Duke of Edinburgh, the Queen Mother and the Queen's sister, Princess Margaret, all came.

Frances and Johnnie lived at Park House in Norfolk. The Royal Family had a house nearby called Sandringham House. The royals often came to Sandringham on holiday. They knew the Spencer family well.

Johnnie Spencer and Frances Roche at their wedding, 1 June, 1954

When Frances's father died, he left her a lot of money. Frances used the money to buy a farm at Snettisham, near Park House. In 1955 the couple had a daughter, Sarah, and in 1957, another daughter, Jane.

In 1960, they had another child. This time it was a boy, called John. But he died after only ten hours.

Then, on the 1st of July 1961, Diana was born. And three years later, in May 1964, Frances and Johnnie had a boy, Charles. But there were problems in the marriage. In 1966 Frances met a new man, Peter Shand Kydd, at a party in London. Frances and Peter fell in love.

At Christmas 1967, Frances left Johnnie and moved to London. She wanted to take the children with her. Johnnie wanted them to stay at Park House with him.

Diana missed her mother very much. She was only six years old when Frances left. Her sisters were at boarding school – a type of school where they lived most of the time. It was a sad and very difficult time for Diana and Charles.

After Frances left, Johnnie paid money to different women – called nannies – to look after the children at Park House. The Spencer children loved Park House. It was a large and friendly house. Diana loved animals like dogs, cats and rabbits. She enjoyed swimming, playing tennis, and going for picnics on the beach. She visited her mother in London at the weekends.

Sometimes the Royal Family invited the Spencer children to the big house at Sandringham. Diana was good friends with Prince Charles's younger brother, Prince Andrew.

Diana's mother and father divorced in April 1969. Frances married Peter Shand Kydd soon after. Diana and her brother had holidays with Peter and his three children. Later, Frances and Peter bought a big house on the Isle of Seil. Seil was an island near the west coast of Scotland.

The Spencer family at Althorp House, 1969. Diana (left) and Charles are at the front of the picture

Diana went to a small day school near her home called Silfield. But when she was nine, her father sent her to boarding school. The school was called Riddlesworth Hall.

In September 1973, when Diana was twelve, she moved to another school called West Heath. West Heath was near the town of Sevenoaks in Kent. Diana liked her new school. She had some good friends there. She learned to dance and play the piano. She was not very interested in school exams, but she was good at dancing and swimming.

At this time, Johnnie Althorp met a new woman. Her name was Raine Legge, the Countess of Dartmouth. Raine was also the writer Barbara Cartland's daughter.

Raine was married with four children. Johnnie's children loved their father very much and they did not want him to be with another woman.

Then, on the 9th of June 1975, Johnnie's father, Jack, died. Jack was the seventh Earl Spencer. Now Johnnie became the eighth Earl Spencer and Diana became 'Lady Diana Spencer'. Johnnie and his family went to live in his father's great house at Althorp in Northampton.

The Spencer children did not like Althorp very much. It was a very big house in a large park. It had 121 rooms. It was a beautiful house but it was also very cold. It was not a 'home' like Park House.

Raine started to come to Althorp a lot. In May 1976, Raine and her husband divorced. Two months later, in July, Johnnie and Raine married quietly in London. Johnnie did not tell his children about the wedding. They read about it in the newspapers.

The Spencer children were very angry with their father. Now Raine lived at Althorp all the time. Diana loved her father, but he was now married to Raine. This was very difficult for Diana.

Johnnie Spencer and his second wife Raine in front of Althorp House, 1 January, 1981

Many of Raine and Johnnie's friends visited Althorp. They had a lot of parties there. But the Spencer girls were always cold to Raine. In 1978, Johnnie was very ill and was close to death. Raine looked after him and helped save his life. Johnnie was lucky and he got better. But still the children did not like Raine.

2

The Prince

Prince Charles was born on the 14th of November 1948 at Buckingham Palace. He is the oldest of the Queen's four children. He is also the Prince of Wales. After the

King or Queen dies, the Prince of Wales usually becomes king. So Charles is 'heir to the throne', or the next king.

When he was a boy, Charles was very shy. He went first to a day school in London. Later his parents sent him to Gordonstoun, a boarding school in north-east Scotland. Life for Charles at Gordonstoun was very hard. Charles was sad there and did not have any friends. He did not see his parents very often.

Later, Charles went to Cambridge University. Then he was an officer in the Royal Navy – the part of the armed forces that works at sea. He was in the navy for five years. He was a pilot and flew planes and helicopters.

Charles enjoyed horse riding, and loved playing polo – a game for people riding on horses. He also liked hunting and shooting animals, for example birds and deer, with a gun.

Prince Charles playing polo in Kenya, February 1971

When Charles was twenty-three, in the summer of 1970, he met Camilla Shand at a polo match. Camilla was fifteen months older than Charles. Camilla was pretty and fun. She liked the same things as Charles. She loved horses, dogs, the countryside and hunting.

Charles and Camilla spent weekends together at the home of Earl Mountbatten. Earl Mountbatten was Charles's father's uncle. Charles was very close to Earl Mountbatten. He called the Earl 'Grandpa'.

But Camilla married another young man called Andrew Parker Bowles in July 1973. After that, Charles had many girlfriends. The newspapers started calling him 'the Playboy Prince'.

Charles liked tall, blonde women. Some of his girlfriends were Davina Sheffield, Anna Wallace and Mountbatten's granddaughter, Amanda Knatchbull.

Charles also had friends who were married women. One of these was an Australian woman called Dale Tryon (her friends called her 'Kanga', like the Australian animal 'kangeroo').

But the most important woman friend for Charles was still Camilla Parker Bowles.

Camilla and Andrew Parker Bowles were now married with two children. Andrew Parker Bowles knew about his wife's friendship with Prince Charles, but he was not unhappy about it. In fact, Andrew and Prince Charles were friends.

Then something exciting happened. Sarah Spencer, Diana's older sister, met Prince Charles at a party at

Windsor Castle in the summer of 1977. She went to watch the Prince playing polo. Later, they went on a skiing holiday together. The Queen invited Sarah to Balmoral, the Royal Family's Scottish home.

That November, Sarah invited Prince Charles to Althorp for the weekend. Diana was there too. She first met Prince Charles in the countryside near her home. She was just sixteen years old.

In April 1978, Diana's sister, Jane, got married. Her husband was Robert Fellowes, the son of a Norfolk family. Later, Robert Fellowes had a very important job. He was private secretary to the Queen – helping her and working very closely with her.

Sarah's romance with Prince Charles ended. On the 14th of November 1978 the Prince had a dance for his thirtieth birthday at Buckingham Palace. He invited Sarah but he invited Diana too. Diana was very surprised and excited. She liked Prince Charles very much.

Mountbatten wanted Charles to marry and have children. Charles usually listened to Mountbatten, but he did not want to get married. He did not need a wife. He liked painting pictures and he liked reading books. He had his girlfriends. He also had servants – or people who worked for him – to do things for him.

Then in 1979 the IRA (Irish Republican Army) killed Earl Mountbatten with a bomb in his fishing boat. Mountbatten was dead and Charles was shocked and very sad. 'I have lost someone very special in my life,' he said.

3

The Fairy Story Begins

Diana was now a young woman of seventeen. She wanted to go and live in London. Both her sisters, Sarah and Jane, lived there. They worked for *Vogue* magazine. But Diana was not interested in a job that paid lots of money. She loved children and was very good with them. So she went to London and found jobs looking after children.

Diana was very happy with her new life. Her mother, Frances, had a flat in Cadogan Square – a very wealthy part of London. Diana lived in the flat with two girlfriends. In July 1979 her mother bought her a flat in London for her eighteenth birthday. The address was 60 Coleherne Court, Chelsea. Diana lived there with three friends – Carolyn Pride (or Carolyn Bartholomew after she was married), Anne Bolton and Virginia Pitman.

Diana enjoyed London. She did not like parties, but sometimes she went to dances at country houses. But she liked sitting at home and watching television with her girlfriends.

In May 1980, Diana's sister, Sarah, married Neil McCorquodale, an officer in the army. The married couple lived in Chelsea too, near Diana. Diana often went to Sarah's house. Sometimes Sarah paid Diana to clean her house for her.

Diana was now nineteen years old. She was a happy, pretty young woman. Life was good for her.

Diana met Charles again in July 1980 at a house party in West Sussex. He invited her to go with him on the royal yacht – a large boat called *Britannia*. They were on the boat at Cowes in the Isle of Wight, an island off the south of England. Later, in September, Prince Charles invited Diana to stay at Balmoral in Scotland. He invited some other friends, too, but they were all much older than Diana. Diana's sister, Jane, and her husband, Robert Fellowes, were there. Camilla and Andrew Parker Bowles were there too.

Charles started seeing Diana more and more. The newspapers were very interested in Charles's romantic life. Soon, they knew all about his beautiful new girlfriend. One story in *The Sun* newspaper said, 'He's in love again! Lady Di is the New Girl for Charles!'

The newspaper reporters – the people who write the stories for newspapers – came to Diana's flat at 60 Coleherne Court in London. They waited outside. All the reporters wanted to take photographs of her. Diana was always nice to the reporters. The reporters liked her, and became her friends. The newspapers started calling her 'Shy Di'.

On the 14th of November 1980 Charles was thirty-two years old. The newspapers and Charles's family asked the same question – 'Is Prince Charles going to marry Lady Diana?'

In January 1981 Charles went on a skiing holiday to Klosters in Switzerland. When he was there, he telephoned Diana. 'I've got something to ask you,' he said. Diana was very excited. She sat with her girlfriends very late at night talking about Prince Charles.

When Charles returned from his holiday, he asked Diana to marry him. Diana said, 'yes'. On the 24th of February 1981, Buckingham Palace told the country that Charles, Prince of Wales, was going to marry Lady Diana Spencer. Charles and Diana gave a television interview in the garden of Buckingham Palace.

'Can you find the right words to say how you feel today?' asked the interviewer.

'Difficult to find the right sort of words,' said Charles. 'Just delighted and happy ...'

'And I suppose in love?' asked the interviewer.

'Of course,' said Diana shyly.

'Whatever "in love" means,' Charles answered.

Two nights later, Diana went to live at Buckingham Palace.

Most people in Britain were very happy about Charles and Diana. People liked reading about Charles's girlfriends, but now it was time for him to marry. Everyone was excited about the royal wedding.

Many people thought that Diana was the perfect wife for Charles. She was a beautiful young girl – tall and blonde. She was very sweet and shy. And – very importantly for the Royal Family – Prince Charles was her first boyfriend. Because of this, the newspapers could not write stories about Diana and other boyfriends.

Camilla was also happy about Diana. Camilla was married and had a husband, Andrew Parker Bowles. She could not be Charles's wife. But Charles was going to be the next king. He needed to have children, so he had to marry someone. And Diana was a very sweet girl.

Diana found her new life at Buckingham palace lonely and a little difficult. She had to meet lots of new people and learn new things. Charles invited Diana to his friends' homes. Often Camilla was there too. Camilla often talked to Diana about Charles. Diana was very surprised. Why was Camilla always there? And how did she know so much about Charles?

Charles and Diana were married on the 29th of July 1981. It was a beautiful summer's day. It was a perfect, romantic wedding. Seven hundred and fifty million people in more than seventy countries watched the wedding on television. 'Lady Di' was now 'Princess Di'. She was not a shy young girl now, she was a Princess.

Diana looked beautiful at her wedding. She was in love with her husband and she was very happy. She wore a wonderful long dress of expensive silk. Later, after the wedding, the new couple kissed outside Buckingham Palace. People all around the world watched the kiss and were happy for Charles and Diana. And thousands of people waited in the streets of London. They wanted to see the royal couple.

After the wedding, Charles and Diana went to Broadlands – Mountbatten's country home – for two days. Then they went on honeymoon – the holiday after a wedding – on the royal yacht Britannia. But it was not a very private honeymoon. There were two hundred sailors

Prince Charles and Princess Diana at their wedding, 29 July, 1981

working on the ship too. So Charles and Diana were not alone very much.

Charles liked reading books written by his friend, the South African writer Laurens van der Post. He brought some of van der Post's books with him on the honeymoon. He sat on the boat reading them. Diana was not interested in these books, so she talked to the sailors and cooks.

Later, in September of that year, Charles and Diana went on holiday to Balmoral, in Scotland. The Queen, the Duke of Edinburgh and the Queen Mother were there too. Diana liked Scotland, but she did not like the same things as Charles and other people in his family. She did not like hunting and shooting animals. Diana did not feel part of the family.

In October Charles and Diana went to Wales for their first public visit. Newspaper and television reporters came from all over the world to take pictures of Diana. They were very interested in the new Princess of Wales.

Diana did not feel well. She was pregnant with her first baby. But she got out of the car and walked in the streets to meet people. She knew how to talk to people. She talked to children and old people. And she talked in public for the first time. She made this speech in Welsh, the national language of Wales.

Everyone loved Diana. They shouted, 'We want Di! We want Di! We want Di!' The people were more interested in Diana than in her husband, Prince Charles.

On the 21st of June 1982 Diana and Charles's first son, Prince William, was born. Prince Charles was with Diana at the hospital all day. When William was born, Charles was very happy.

It was only eleven months after the royal wedding. Diana was not a young, shy girl living in a flat with friends now. She was a royal wife. And she was mother of the future King. It was a big change in Diana's life.

Everybody was very excited about the baby prince. Diana and Charles arrived home from the hospital and the crowds of people waved and shouted. It was a happy time for the princess.

4

'We want Di!'

Charles and Diana had a new London home. This home was an apartment, or flat, in Kensington Palace. Some other members of the Royal Family had apartments in Kensington Palace too. The Queen's sister, Princess Margaret, lived there. Princess Margaret had a party for Charles and Diana and the baby.

Charles also had a house in Gloucestershire, in the west of England. This house was called Highgrove. It was near the home of Camilla and Andrew Parker Bowles. Charles and Camilla often went hunting together in the countryside near Highgrove.

After Prince William was born, Diana became ill. She began to have problems with eating. She had an illness called 'bulimia nervosa'. She often ate a lot of food, then made herself sick. Charles was worried about his wife. But he did not understand her problems.

Diana started to look unwell. She became very thin. Some newspaper reporters began to ask questions about her health. Diana read these stories in the newspapers and she became very unhappy.

In March 1983, Charles and Diana went to visit different places in Australia. They took the baby Prince William with them. This tour of Australia was very successful. It was the beginning of 'Di-Mania' – everybody was crazy about Diana. Everybody loved her and wanted to see her. Hundreds of photographers came from countries all over the world. They all wanted photos of Diana for their newspapers.

Charles and Diana visited many of Australia's cities. Almost one million people came to see them. In each city Charles and Diana did a 'walkabout' – they walked in the crowded city streets and talked to the people. But the people wanted to see Diana more than Charles. 'We want Di!' they shouted.

Later that year, Charles and Diana went on a tour of Canada. This tour was also a big success. But again, the people's favourite was Diana, not Charles. This was very difficult for Charles.

Diana meets the crowds in New Zealand, April, 1983

Diana was very good at talking to people. She talked to people of all ages – old and young. She talked to sick people too. When she smiled at people, they felt happy. A newspaper in America wrote, 'Diana is the most popular woman in the world'. The French magazine, *Paris-Match*, wrote, 'Diana is more popular than [the actress] Brigitte Bardot'.

Charles and Diana went on holiday in April 1983 to the Bahamas. The photographers took pictures of them on a beach. Charles and Diana walked hand in hand. They looked happy and in love.

Diana became pregnant again. On the 15th of September 1984, the baby was born. It was another boy. His name was Prince Henry Charles Albert David. Everyone called him 'Prince Harry'. Now William had a brother.

Soon after Harry was born, Diana started to work for charities – groups which help people in need. She became president of Barnardo's, the children's charity. She visited Barnardo's children's homes all over the UK (United Kingdom) and talked to people there. Some people in Barnardo's had very sad lives. They felt better when they talked to Diana about their problems. And Diana was good at listening to their stories.

The newspapers loved writing about Diana's clothes and hair. When the Queen opened Parliament one year, the newspapers were not very interested. Diana's clothes were more important!

In 1985, Charles and Diana went on tours to Italy, Australia and the USA (the United States of America). In America, Charles and Diana visited President Reagan and his wife, Nancy. President Reagan gave a big dance for the couple. Diana wore a beautiful black dress and danced with the famous actor, John Travolta. She looked very happy.

Diana was no longer 'Shy Di'. She was beautiful and she could dress well. She had a wonderful smile. But she also cared about people. She talked to them and made them happy. Everyone loved her.

But at this time some reporters started writing about problems in Charles and Diana's marriage. They said that there were big differences between Charles and Diana. 'Diana is a very young twenty-four, Charles is a very old thirty-six,' wrote one newspaper.

5

The Problems Begin

Diana was the wife of Prince Charles and the mother of Princes William and Harry. She was a very important person. So a policeman had to go everywhere with her. This policeman's job was to protect Diana and look after her. When Diana walked in the park, the policeman went with her. When she went shopping or out in the evenings, he went too.

The Princess became very close to one policeman, Barry Manakee. When she took William and Harry out, Manakee went too. The newspapers showed many photographs of Diana with her sons and Barry Manakee.

Some people began to think, 'Princess Diana is in love with Barry Manakee'. This was not good for Prince Charles or the Royal Family. So Manakee lost his job of looking after the Princess. Two years later, Manakee died in a motorbike accident.

Another new person came into Diana's life. This was Sarah Ferguson, usually called 'Fergie'. Sarah was older than Diana. Her father, Ronald Ferguson, was Prince Charles's polo manager – the person who trains the polo team. Sarah and Diana first met at a polo match. Sarah lived in a flat in London with friends. She had lots of red hair and loved having fun. Sarah and Diana started having lunch together every week.

Diana invited Fergie to dinner at Kensington Palace. There she met Prince Charles's younger brother, Prince Andrew. Fergie and Andrew fell in love. They married on 23rd July 1986, in another big royal wedding.

Diana and Fergie were friends. But Fergie was very different from Diana. She loved outdoor life and sports. She was very good at riding and she loved horses. She enjoyed going to Balmoral, and doing things outdoors with the Royal Family.

Charles and Diana were very different kinds of people. Charles was not interested in the same things as Diana. He could not understand her. He could not understand her problems with bulimia, or that she needed help.

Charles started seeing many of his old friends again. He spent a lot of time with Camilla Parker Bowles. Camilla understood Charles, and made him feel good. She was not difficult, like Diana.

Diana knew that Charles was spending time with Camilla. She became angry and jealous. She felt that her husband did not love her any more. So she started to see a young army officer. His name was James Hewitt.

Diana and Hewitt met at a polo game. Hewitt was very good looking. He was kind, and could talk to women easily. He was good at listening too. Later they met again at Buckingham Palace. Diana asked Hewitt to give her horse riding lessons.

James Hewitt in London, 11 March, 2004

Hewitt cared about Diana, and made her feel good. Diana told Hewitt about her bulimia and he listened. They spent weekends together at Highgrove. Sometimes they went to Hewitt's mother's house in Devon, in the south-west of England.

Sometimes Charles liked going to places by himself. He wanted to be alone and think. In 1987, he went to the Kalahari Desert in Botswana with his friend, the writer Laurens van der Post. Then he went to a lonely island in Scotland. People did not like this. 'Why isn't Charles with Diana?' they asked.

In September the newspapers showed photos of Charles at Balmoral. But Diana was not with him. She was in London with William and Harry. 'Charles and Diana are not speaking,' said the newspapers. People began to ask questions about the royal marriage. Were Charles and Diana not happy?

Diana did more charity work. She did a lot of work for the old people's charity, Help the Aged, and for people with AIDS (acquired immune deficiency syndrome). She worked hard, and children and old people loved her. Diana was not afraid of people with AIDS. One time, she shook hands with an AIDS patient. The next day, there were photographs in all the newspapers. They called her 'caring Di'.

Two years later, she visited the Harlem Hospital Center in New York. The photographers took a picture of Diana and a child with AIDS. After that, many people heard about the Harlem Hospital. They became interested in the children with AIDS there. So Diana's visit was a very good thing for the hospital.

Now people were not just interested in Diana's clothes or hair. They were interested in her work as well.

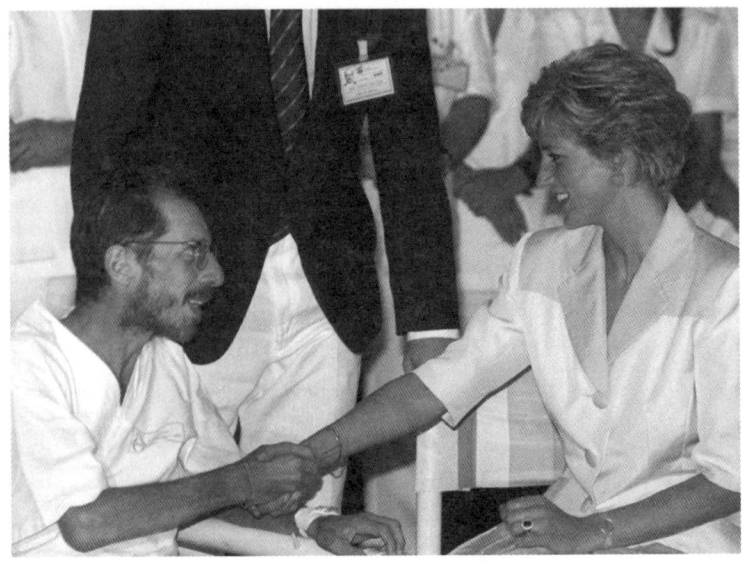

Princess Diana shakes the hand of an AIDS patient in Brazil

6

Unhappy Times

In January 1988 Charles and Diana went on another visit to Australia. Again, everyone wanted to see Diana, not Charles. Diana sang Australia's national song. But Charles did not know the words. 'We love Di!' shouted the people. Charles felt jealous of his wife. It was a difficult time for their marriage.

Diana's mother, Frances Shand Kydd, knew about Diana's problems in her marriage. She tried to help her daughter. But in the summer of 1988, Frances's husband, Peter Shand Kydd, left her. Frances was very sad. Diana invited her mother to Kensington Palace in London. But Frances did not come. She did not want to leave her home in Scotland.

In November 1988 Charles and Diana went to Paris. This visit was very successful. Diana looked beautiful and Charles made speeches in French. Then, on the 14th of November 1988, there was a big dance at Buckingham Palace for Charles's fortieth birthday.

In the autumn of 1989 James Hewitt went to work in Germany. Diana did not want him to go. At this time she met a new male friend, James Gilbey. Gilbey's job was selling expensive cars. Diana and James Gilbey began to meet in London. On New Year's Eve, the 31st of December 1989 someone recorded Diana and James Gilbey talking on the telephone. Gilbey said, 'I love you'. Diana did not know about the recording.

Fergie and Prince Andrew also had problems in their marriage. Andrew was often away for a long time with his job in the navy. Fergie went to Australia for six weeks. There she met a handsome American, Steve Wyatt.

James Hewitt returned to England and then went with the army to Iraq. While he was in Iraq, Diana telephoned him. She sent him letters and expensive food. In 1991 some newspaper reporters started writing about Diana and James Hewitt. Diana did not want people to find out about her relationship with Hewitt. When Hewitt came back from Iraq, she did not see him.

Diana was very sad and felt very alone. 'What can I do?' she thought.

She decided to tell the public about her life. She wanted people to know her story. But she could not do this alone. So she asked a reporter, Andrew Morton, to help her. She asked him to write a book about her life. She wanted him to talk to her friends. But she did not tell anyone in the Royal Family about the book. It was a secret.

Many newspaper reporters liked Diana and felt sorry for her. Sometimes Diana took William and Harry to amusement parks – large parks which have rides and many different fun activities. She also took them on a skiing holiday to Austria. But Charles did not go with them. 'Where is Charles?' asked the newspapers. 'Diana is a loving mother, but Charles is a bad father.'

In June 1991 William had an accident at his school. A golf ball hit him on the head. Charles and Diana took William to the Great Ormond Street Hospital for Sick Children in London. William needed an operation. Diana stayed with William at the hospital all night but Charles left. 'What kind of father are you?' asked the newspapers the next day.

On 1st July 1991 Diana was thirty years old. The 29th of July was Charles and Diana's 10th wedding anniversary. But their marriage was not a happy one.

7

A Terrible Year

1992 was a very bad year for the Royal Family.

In January, holiday photographs of Fergie and Steve Wyatt appeared in the newspapers. The British people were shocked. Fergie's marriage to Prince Andrew was finished. Wyatt went back to America. Then Fergie became friends with an American called John Bryan.

In February, Charles and Diana went to India. Photographers took pictures of Diana, in front of the Taj Mahal.

The history of the Taj Mahal is very romantic. An Indian emperor built it for his dead wife. Diana sat in front of it, alone. Charles was at a business meeting.

On 29th March, Diana's father, Johnnie, died suddenly. Diana was on a skiing holiday with Charles and the boys in Austria. Her father's death was a terrible shock. Charles and Diana flew back to London. On the 1st of April, Diana drove to Althorp for the funeral – the ceremony for a dead person – and Charles came later by helicopter.

Diana did not like Raine, Johnnie's wife. But at the funeral, she spoke to Raine and held her hand. After this, Diana's relationship with Raine was better.

Andrew Morton's book about Diana was ready. He called it *Diana: Her True Story*. Diana wanted the British people to know the truth about her life. But now she was worried. The Royal Family did not know anything about the book. Perhaps the book was not a good idea.

On the 7th of June 1992 the *Sunday Times* newspaper printed a part of Andrew Morton's book. For the first time, people read about Diana's bulimia. They read about Charles and Camilla. They learned how Charles was cold to Diana. Now people could not believe in the royal fairy story. They were very shocked.

The British people began to dislike Prince Charles. 'Charles is a bad husband and not a very good father,' they said. 'He doesn't care about Diana. He only cares about himself and Camilla Parker Bowles.'

The Royal Family asked questions. 'Andrew Morton did not write this book alone,' they said. 'So Diana's friends talked to him. But did Diana know about this book?' The husband of Diana's sister, Jane, was Robert Fellowes, private secretary to the Queen. 'Did you know about Andrew Morton's book?' he asked Diana. 'No,' replied Diana. Fellowes believed her. But later, he found out the truth.

Diana became more popular because of Andrew Morton's book. At the end of June 1992, she went to Belfast in Northern Ireland. 'We want Di! We want Di!' shouted the people.

In August 1992 *The Sun* newspaper printed stories about Diana and James Gilbey, and Diana and James Hewitt. Later, Diana and Charles went to Korea but the visit was not successful. Charles and Diana did not look happy together. In November, Diana went to Paris alone.

The problems between Charles and Diana grew worse. On the 25th of November they met at Kensington Palace and talked about a separation. On the 9th of December, the Prime Minister, John Major, gave a speech to the British Parliament. 'The Prince and Princess of Wales, have decided to separate,' he said. But they had 'no plans to divorce'.

In her Christmas speech at the end of the year, the Queen called 1992 a 'horrible' year for the Royal Family.

8

Princess Alone

Diana was now alone and she wanted a normal, private life. Because she was the Princess of Wales, she had a policeman with her all the time. But now Diana decided she did not need a policeman.

Without a policeman, it was easy for the newspaper reporters and photographers to follow her. They waited for her outside Kensington Palace. They waited for her when she went out in London. They waited for her at airports when she went on holiday.

Diana's sons, Prince William and Prince Harry, were the centre of her life. Diana was a very good mother. She wanted William and Harry to have a normal life and to have fun like other children. So she took them out to the cinema, or McDonalds, or shopping. She did not want them to see only rich people like the Royal Family. She wanted them to meet people in the normal world too – people with sad and difficult lives.

She took William to The Passage Day Centre in London. The centre was a place for people who live on the streets. William met the people there and talked to them. William was only a young boy, but he was like Diana. He was very good at talking to people. Later, Diana took Harry to the centre for homeless people too.

When William and Harry were at home with her, Diana spent a lot of time with them. But most of the time they were away at boarding school. Then Diana was lonely at home by herself.

Diana soon met a new man, Oliver Hoare. Oliver Hoare was very good-looking and popular. He knew a lot about art, and bought and sold Islamic art. He was married. Oliver and his wife were friends of Prince Charles. Hoare and Diana talked to each other on the phone and met at Diana's friends' houses.

Diana was still doing her charity work. In March 1993 she visited Nepal. In July, she visited Zimbabwe. She visited a hospital where there were children with AIDS. The children were only five years old but they had no parents. Diana cried when she saw them. She went to the countryside and gave food to poor and hungry children.

At home, Diana became interested in women's problems. In April 1993, she gave a speech about eating problems in young women.

The newspapers were still very interested in Diana. She had very little private life and this was very hard for

Princess Diana visiting Niagara Falls with William and Harry, 26 October, 1991

her. At a dinner on the 3rd of December 1993, at the Dorchester Hotel in London, she made a speech. She said the newspaper and television reporters made her life very difficult. She had no private life and needed more time alone. She did not want to do so many things in public. She did not want to do so much charity work.

Oliver Hoare left his wife. But in January 1994 he went back to her. He did not want to leave his family for

33

Diana. Then, in March, James Hewitt gave an interview to a reporter from the *Daily Express*. The newspaper printed the story of Hewitt's relationship with Diana. Now the British people knew about Diana's relationship with Hewitt. Later that year, Hewitt published a book about his time with Diana. The book was called *Princess in Love*.

People already knew about Diana's story from Andrew Morton's book. They felt very sorry for her. This made Charles very angry. So he decided to tell the British people about his life too. He asked a journalist, Jonathan Dimbleby, to write a biography – a book about Charles's life. He also did an interview with Jonathan Dimbleby on television.

Many of Charles's friends did not want him to do the interview. 'It is not a good idea for the Prince to talk about his personal life on television,' they said. But Charles did not listen to his friends.

The interview was on television on the 29th of June 1994. Charles talked about the British countryside and about his work with young people. But he also talked about a relationship with another woman. People thought this woman was Camilla Parker Bowles. Millions of people watched the interview. They were very shocked. While Charles was married to Diana, he had a girlfriend!

Seven months later, Andrew and Camilla Parker Bowles divorced.

9

The Road to Divorce

Diana went to the United States in October 1994. The American people liked her very much. Her visit was very successful. She met important people like Hillary Clinton and General Colin Powell. She talked to Hillary about her children, and her plans for the future.

Soon Diana returned to London. She started her charity work again. She visited two special hospitals for people with mental problems. Later in 1994, she went to see people in the poor parts of Paris. At the end of her visit, the French President, President Mitterand, gave a dinner for her at the Palace of Versailles. He invited nine hundred people.

Diana was not with her husband now, but she had some very good friends. These friends helped her a lot.

One very close friend was Lucia Flecha de Lima. Lucia lived in Washington with her husband. But she spoke to Diana a lot on the telephone. She gave Diana advice and helped her.

Other good friends were Lady Annabel Goldsmith, Rosa Monckton and Carolyn Bartholomew, her old flatmate.

In 1995 Diana visited ten countries around the world. All of her visits were very successful. One was to Japan. Diana made a speech to the people in Japanese.

Later Diana went to Hong Kong. She raised a quarter of a million pounds for charities for young people and for medical work.

Diana also went to Italy, France, New York, Russia and Argentina. In 1994, Diana made only ten public visits. But in 1995, she made one hundred and twenty seven.

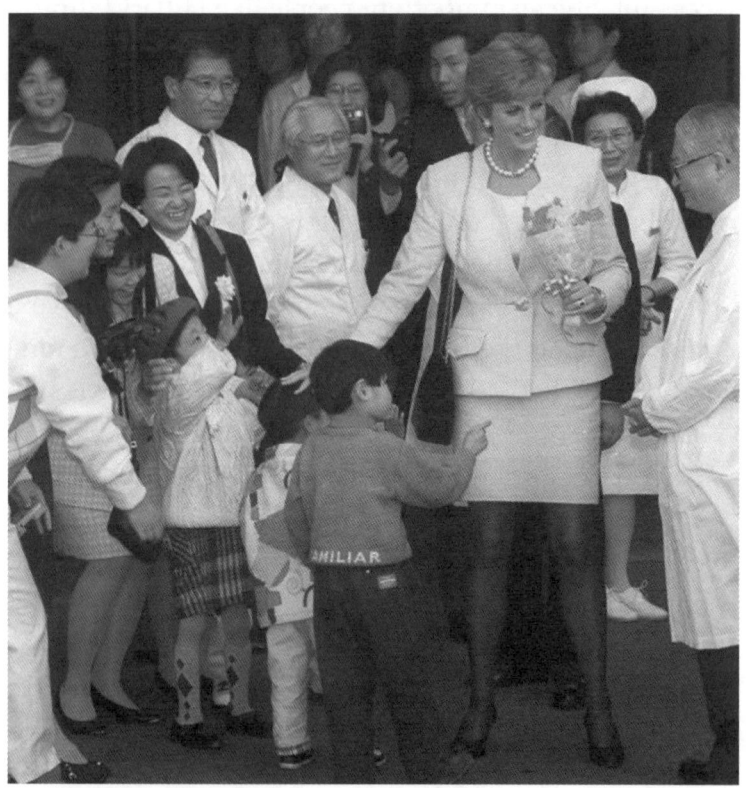

Princess Diana meets the crowds in Tokyo, February 1995

Diana's relationship with Oliver Hoare was over. The newspapers started to write stories about a new male friend. This was Will Carling, an English rugby player and captain of the England rugby team. People were shocked. Diana was liked another married man?

In 1995 Diana met Martin Bashir, a well-known journalist. Bashir worked for the BBC's television programme, *Panorama*. He wanted Diana to do an interview on television. The BBC showed the interview on the 20th of November 1995. Diana looked beautiful but sad. She wore black clothes and black make-up round her eyes.

Diana talked about her relationship with Charles and the Royal Family. She talked about Camilla Parker Bowles. 'There were three of us in this marriage,' she said. She talked about Andrew Morton's book, her bulimia and her relationship with James Hewitt. 'I want to help people with problems,' she said.

Fifteen million people in Britain watched the interview. Millions of other people round the world watched it too. They were shocked.

Diana's friends thought the interview was a terrible mistake. The Royal Family were also very upset. After the interview, Princess Margaret did not want to be friends with Diana any more.

In December 1995 Diana had a letter from the Queen. The Queen wanted Charles and Diana to divorce. She was worried about her country and the Royal Family. Later, on the 15th of February 1996, Diana met the Queen at Buckingham Palace. 'I do not want a divorce,' said Diana, 'I still love Charles.' Diana and the Queen talked about William and Harry, and about Diana's future.

Later in February 1996, Diana met with Prince Charles. They talked about the end of their marriage. On the 28th of August 1996, they were divorced. After the divorce, Diana lost her title 'Her Royal Highness' and her special place in the Royal Family. She was now just 'Diana, Princess of Wales'.

'I never wanted a divorce,' Diana wrote. 'I always dreamed of a happy marriage.'

But the fairy-tale marriage was over.

10

Starting a New Life

Diana was alone and she had to make a new life for herself.

She knew many rich and famous people. But she did not only want to spend time with them. She wanted a normal life. And she wanted to help the poor and the sick.

Diana had many beautiful dresses and other clothes. But she did not need these clothes now. They were from her old life with Prince Charles. She did not want to wear them again. But she did not know what to do with them. Then Prince William had a good idea. 'Sell the clothes and make money for charity, ' he said.

Christie's, a famous auction house, helped Diana. At an auction, a lot of people come to see things that are for sale. The person who offers the most money for an object can buy it. In September 1996, a person from *Christie's* went to see Diana at Kensington Palace. They talked about the sale of Diana's clothes at an auction. Diana wanted the sale to be in New York. She wanted the money to help people with AIDS.

Diana also wanted to help people in other countries. She was very worried about landmines. A landmine is a bomb which is put under the ground. It explodes when a person or car moves over it. Many countries use landmines in wars. Landmines are very dangerous. People, often women and children, die or lose arms or legs because of landmines.

Many people did not know about landmines and Diana wanted to tell the world about them. She wanted to stop countries from using landmines in war. She talked to the British Red Cross and, in January 1997, she went to Angola for the Red Cross. There was terrible war in Angola and there were many landmines in that country.

People who worked for the television company the BBC went with Diana and filmed her. She met people with terrible landmine injuries. She worked hard and visited dangerous places. She walked in parts of the countryside where there were landmines. But she was not afraid.

She went to hospitals and talked to children with injuries from landmines. She sat with them and held their hands.

Diana also wanted to help people with eating problems. In the UK, in May 1997, she made a speech. 'I don't have problems with bulimia any more,' she said.

Princess Diana meets landmine victims in Angola, 15 January, 1997

Diana looked beautiful and healthy.

Diana was very busy. In May, she and Prince William went to lunch with the new British Prime Minister, Tony Blair, and his family. They talked about Diana's future. In June, Diana flew to Washington to meet Hillary Clinton. Then she went to New York to meet Mother Teresa. She liked Mother Teresa's work very much.

Later that year, in June, she flew back to New York for a party at Christie's auction house. The party was before the sale of Diana's clothes. The sale was a great success. All Diana's dresses sold for a total of $3,258,750. The top price was $222,500 for a dress. Diana wore this dress when she danced with John Travolta.

11

New Love

There was a new man in Diana's life.

Diana knew a woman called Oonagh Shanley-Toffolo. Oonagh's husband, Joseph, had a problem with his heart. In August 1995, he was very ill. He went to the Royal Brompton Hospital in London. He had a heart operation.

On August the 31st Oonagh telephoned Diana. Diana went quickly to the hospital. She met Joseph's doctors. One of them was Hasnat Khan. Hasnat Khan was from Pakistan. He was thirty-six years old and very good-looking.

Diana often went to the hospital. She met Hasnat Khan many times. She was very interested in his work. Sometimes she watched him doing operations. Diana and Hasnat Khan were good friends. Soon they became more than friends.

Diana often called Hasnat Khan at the hospital. But when she called him, she did not use her real name. Sometimes she called herself Dr Armani. Sometimes Diana and Hasnat Khan had dinner in small restaurants in London. But Khan usually came to Kensington Palace. Diana was very happy.

Diana was very much in love with Hasnat Khan. Khan cared about people and he saved lives. Diana liked this. She began reading medical books so she could talk to him about his work. Khan was also very kind to her. And he liked Diana the person, not because she was a Princess.

Hasnat Khan's religion was Islam. So Diana also began reading books about Islam. And she became very interested in Pakistan. She bought Pakistani women's clothes. Diana's good friend, Lady Annabel Goldsmith, had a young and beautiful daughter, Jemima. Jemima was married to the famous Pakistani cricket player, Imran Khan. Imran Khan was interested in Pakistani politics. He also had a hospital in Pakistan for people with cancer – a serious illness.

Diana became very friendly with Jemima Khan. She talked to her about marriage to a Pakistani man. Diana went to Lahore, Pakistan, in February and May of 1996. She visited Jemima and Imran Khan, and Imran Khan's hospital. She talked to many children with cancer and helped them a lot. Many photographs appeared in the newspapers of Diana with sick children.

At first, Diana and Hasnat's relationship was secret. But later the newspapers found out about it. Hasnat Khan was very unhappy. He did not want the newspapers to write stories about him and Diana. He did not want his photograph in all the newspapers. He did not want to be famous because he was Diana's lover.

Diana wanted to marry Khan. But the most important thing in Hasnat Khan's life was his work. He wanted to be a good doctor and to work in Pakistan, his home country. He did not want to be Diana's husband.

Diana and Khan's relationship finished. Diana still wanted to marry him. But she knew that they had no future.

That same summer, Diana met another man – Dodi Al Fayed.

12

The Last Summer

Dodi Al Fayed's father was Mohammed Al Fayed. Mohammed Al Fayed was Egyptian and he was very rich. He had nine houses, a private plane, a helicopter, many expensive cars and a film company. In 1979, he bought the Ritz hotel in Paris. And in 1984, he bought the most famous shop in London – *Harrods*.

Mohammed Al Fayed liked British people. He wanted to be part of British society. He wanted famous people like Diana to be his friends. So in the summer of 1997, he invited Diana and her sons to stay with him and his family. They could stay at his home near St Tropez, in the south of France.

Diana had no summer plans for herself and her sons. So she said, 'yes' to Mohammed.

Mohammed bought a beautiful yacht, the *Jonikal*. It cost £15 million. Sixteen sailors worked on the boat. Mohammed telephoned his son, Dodi. At that time, Dodi was in Paris with his fiancée – the woman he planned to marry. She was an American model called Kelly Fisher. Mohammed told his son to leave Kelly and come and meet Diana. On the 14th of July he sent his private plane to Paris. the plane took Dodi to the family villa.

Dodi Fayed was forty-two years old. He had the life of a playboy. His father gave him lots of money and he spent it on having fun and driving fast cars. He was also successful with women because he was good-looking and kind.

On the 16th of July, Diana and the boys flew in Mohammed's private plane to France. They stayed in his villa, the Castel Sainte Hélène and spend time on his yacht.

The photographers followed Diana to the south of France. They waited in boats near Mohammed's villa. They took pictures of Diana by the swimming pool and having fun in the sea.

The photographers saw Dodi with Diana. But they did not know who he was. They thought he was a sailor from the *Jonikal*. They did not know he was Mohammed Al Fayed's son. But they saw that Diana looked very happy.

Kelly Fisher, Dodi's fiancée, saw photos of Diana and Dodi in the newspapers. She was very angry. She called Dodi but he did not answer. So she telephoned Dodi's father, Mohammed. But Diana was more important for Mohammed than Kelly.

'Forget about Dodi,' Mohammed told her. 'You and Dodi are finished.'

Diana wrote a letter to Dodi. She thanked him for a

Princess Diana and Dodi in Paris

wonderful holiday together. 'Darling Dodi …' she wrote, 'thank you for the most magical six days on the ocean waves.'

On the 20th of July, Diana flew back to London. There she met Hasnat Khan. But their relationship was finished. In late July, Diana flew back to Paris. She met Dodi for a day. On the 31st of July, she flew back to the *Jonikal*. William and Harry were not with her this time. They were on holiday with Prince Charles in Scotland.

Diana and Dodi went to Corsica and Sardinia on the *Jonikal*. Diana was very happy and relaxed. But the photographers followed them and took photos. The newspapers in London paid a lot of money for these photos.

On the 8th of August Diana went to Bosnia to talk about landmines. She visited Sarajevo and met people with injuries from landmines. Then she went on holiday to Greece with her friend, Rosa Monckton. But Diana and Dodi spent time together, too, in August. They stayed together in London and on the *Jonikal*. The photographers were there all the time. They came when Diana and Dodi had a romantic walk on a beach. They flew in helicopters over the *Jonikal*.

On the 30th of August Diana and Dodi went to Paris. But the photographers found out their plans. The photographers waited for them at the airport. They followed their car on motorbikes, trying to take photographs.

Diana and Dodi went to Dodi's apartment to dress for dinner. The photographers waited outside the apartment, shouting and pushing. Dodi was angry. When Diana and Dodi came out of the apartment, the photographers were still there. They got on their bikes and drove very near the car. It was very dangerous.

A table was reserved for dinner at a restaurant called Chez Benoît. But Dodi did not want the photographers to follow them there. So he changed their plans and decided to have dinner at the Ritz hotel. They drove to the Ritz. But the photographers were there too. Diana got out of the car and ran inside.

Dodi and Diana had dinner upstairs in the Ritz. At dinner, Dodi made a plan to lose the photographers. Dodi's car was at the front door of the hotel. But Dodi decided to use another car at the back door. The photographers did not know about this car.

The assistant head of security at the Ritz was called Henri Paul. Dodi told Henri Paul about his plan. He wanted him to drive the secret car.

Diana and Dodi left by the back door. Trevor Rees-Jones – a man who worked for the Fayeds and protected Diana – went too. Dodi sat in the back behind Henri Paul. Diana was on Dodi's right side. Nobody in the car wore a seat belt. At about midnight, Paul drove quickly away from the hotel.

But the photographers soon saw the car. Quickly, they got onto their motorbikes and followed it. Henri Paul tried to lose the photographers. He did not take the direct road, the Champs-Elysées, back to Dodi's apartment. He decided to drive down the tunnel under the Place d'Alma.

Henri Paul was driving too fast and he had alcohol in his body. Only three minutes after leaving the Ritz hotel, the car crashed into part of the tunnel. Dodi and Paul were killed, but Trevor Rees-Jones and Diana were still alive.

About ten to fifteen photographers arrived in seconds and started taking photographs of Diana. Only two of them called for help on their mobile phones. People were very shocked because the photographers did not help the people in the car. When the police arrived, they arrested seven of the photographers.

A doctor, Frédéric Mailliez, was in the tunnel. He

The Paris tunnel where Henri Paul's car crashed

tried to help Diana. Diana did not look badly hurt. But the injuries inside her body were terrible.

The ambulances arrived. They took Diana to La Pitié-Salpêtrière Hospital. But the doctors there could not save her. At 4 am Paris time, on the morning of the 31st of August 1997, Diana died.

The British Ambassador in Paris, Sir Michael Jay, came to the hospital. He telephoned the Queen's assistant private secretary, Sir Robin Janvrin, in London. 'Diana is dead,' he said. Janvrin told the Queen and Prince Philip.

13

The People's Princess

People all over the world heard the sad and terrible news. But nobody could believe it. How could Diana be dead? It could not be true.

Princes William and Harry were at Balmoral, in Scotland, with Prince Charles and the Queen and Prince Philip. Prince Charles told them about their mother's death.

Tony Blair was the new British Prime Minister. The morning after Diana's death, he spoke about Diana and the British people.

'They liked her, they loved her … as one of the people,' he said. 'She was the People's Princess and that's how she will stay … in all our hearts and memories for ever.'

Prince Charles and Diana's two sisters, Sarah and Jane, flew to Paris. They brought Diana's body back to London. Sarah wanted a quiet funeral for Diana at the Spencer family home in Althorp. But thousands of people waited by the road from the airport. There was not going to be a quiet funeral.

Diana's body was taken to the Chapel Royal at St James's Palace. Then it was taken to Kensington Palace. Charles Spencer, Diana's brother, lived in South Africa. He flew to London immediately. Diana's mother, Frances, was at her home in Scotland, on the Isle of Seil. She, too, came to London.

But the Royal Family were still at Balmoral on holiday. The British people began to ask questions. 'Why aren't the Royal Family here in London?' they said. 'Do they care?' said one popular British newspaper, *The Sun*. 'Where is the Queen when the country needs her?' 'Why doesn't the Queen talk to the British people about Diana?' asked the people.

People began to dislike the Royal Family. The Royal Family was cold and did not care about Diana, they said.

People said these things but still the Queen and the Royal Family stayed in Scotland. People put flowers outside the gates of Kensington Palace. The number of flowers grew and grew. People wrote cards and left messages for Diana. They waited for hours to sign a special book to remember Diana.

Then at last, on Friday the 5th of September, the Royal Family returned to London. The Queen made a speech and the family walked in the streets with the people. Finally, they began to understand the feelings of the people.

Diana's funeral was on the 6th of September 1997. More than one million people came to London and many more watched the funeral on television. Prince William and Prince Harry walked behind Diana's coffin – the box where her body was. Diana's favourite white flowers were on top of the coffin. Prince Harry, who was only twelve years old, wrote one word on a card. The word was 'Mummy'. This card was on the coffin too. When people saw the card, they felt very sad.

Princess Diana's funeral, 6 September, 1997

The coffin went from Kensington Palace to Westminster Abbey for the funeral. Thousands of people stood quietly by the road. Many people cried.

Famous people from all over the world came to the funeral service. Bill and Hillary Clinton came. There were actors like Tom Cruise, Tom Hanks and Nicole Kidman. There were singers like Sting, Elton John and George Michael. There were Diana's old school friends like Carolyn Bartholomew and her old headmistress from West Heath school. There were Diana's new friends like Lucia Flecha de Lima. Hasnat Khan was there, and Imran Khan and Jemima. And there were many people from Diana's charities.

Elton John sang a beautiful song, 'Candle in the Wind'. He first wrote it for Marilyn Monroe but wrote new words for Diana. Diana and Marilyn Monroe died at exactly the same age – thirty-six.

Diana's brother, Charles, made a speech at the funeral. 'Diana's name means "huntress",' he said. 'But Diana became the most hunted woman in the world.' Outside thousands of people listened. When Charles finished, they began to clap their hands.

After the funeral, the coffin went very slowly to Althorp, the Spencer family home. People in the streets of London threw flowers. At Althorp, Charles Spencer said, 'Diana is home'.

Diana is now buried in the ground on a small island. The island is in a lake in the garden at Althorp. There are trees all round the lake. It is the perfect place for a princess at peace.

14

After Diana's Death

The Diana, Princess of Wales Memorial Fund

The Diana, Princess of Wales Memorial Fund was started on the 14th of September 1997. When it began, there was £19 million in the fund. Money that Diana left and money from Prince Charles was put into the fund. Money from the people of Britain, and money from the sales of Sir Elton John's song, 'Candle in the Wind', was also put in.

The Fund gives money to people for three reasons. The first reason is to stop the use of landmines, and to help people hurt by landmines. The second is to help people in Africa who are dying from an illness, for example AIDS. The third is to give money to help young people in the UK with special difficulties.

The President of the Fund is Lady Sarah McCorquodale, Diana's oldest sister.

Charles and Camilla

Prince Charles married Camilla Parker Bowles on the 9th of April 2005. After the wedding, the Queen gave a party for Charles and Camilla at Windsor Castle. Later, Charles and Camilla went to Scotland.

Camilla's title is now Her Royal Highness, The Duchess of Cornwall. Sometimes Charles and Camilla carry out royal duties together.

Concert for Diana

On the 1st of July 2007, about ten years after Princess Diana died, there was a concert for her in London. The 1st of July was Diana's birthday.

Prince William and Prince Harry planned the concert. They invited many of the world's most famous singers and entertainers to come there. They invited Sir Elton John, the English National Ballet, Bryan Ferry, Andrea Bocelli, Rod Stewart and Take That.

The concert was eight hours long and was very successful. People in one hundred and forty countries watched the concert on television or heard it on the radio. Sixty-three thousand people came to Wembley Stadium to see the concert. At the end, a video of Diana as a child was shown. The music for the video was the song by the pop group Queen – 'These Are the Days of Our Lives'. There is now a DVD of the concert.

The money from the concert went to charities chosen by Prince William and Prince Harry. The charities were: The Diana, Princess of Wales Memorial Fund; Centrepoint charity for the homeless and Sentebale, a charity started in April 2006 by Prince Harry and Prince Seeiso of Lesotho – a small country in South Africa. This charity helps children and young people in Lesotho. There are many children in Lesotho whose parents have died of AIDS.

———

Diana is dead, but her memory lives on. People all around the world still want to see photographs and read books about her. They still want to know about the beautiful and caring princess who touched people's hearts all over the world.

Exercises

Background information

Choose the correct information to complete the sentences. The first one is done for you.

1   Princess Diana was from Scotland / (England.)

2   She went on holiday in July / August 1997.

3   She was with her new boyfriend / husband.

4   They went to Spain / France.

5   Diana was happy / sad.

6   She was a good / bad mother.

People in the story
Look at the family tree and match the information.

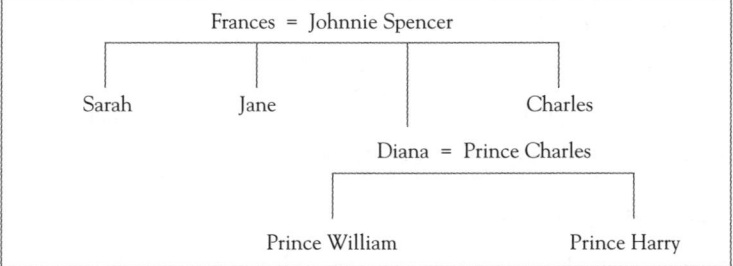

1 Frances is Johnnie's	e	a grandmother
2 Prince William is Diana's		b uncle
3 Jane is Prince Harry's		c grandfather
4 Sarah is Johnnie's		d son
5 Johnnie is Prince William's		e ~~wife~~
6 Prince Charles is Prince Harry's		f husband
7 Charles is Prince William's		g daughter
8 Johnnie is Frances's		h brother

9 Frances is Prince Harry's		i	father
10 Prince William is Prince Harry's		j	grandson
11 Prince William is Johnnie's		k	sister
12 Sarah is Diana's		l	aunt

Grammar: 's

Read the sentences and decide if the *'s* is a *contraction of is* (is) or the *possessive 's* (P)

Example 1: Diana's parents were Johnnie and Frances.	P
Example 2: Prince William's the oldest son.	is

1 Now, Camilla's called Her Royal Highness.   ....

2 Diana's dead but we remember her.   ....

3 Diana's name means 'huntress'.   ....

4 Sir Elton John's song was about Diana.   ....

5 Prince Harry's the second son.   ....

6 Dodi's car was in front of the hotel.   ....

7 Diana's still very popular today.   ....

8 The children didn't like Johnnie's new wife.   ....

Vocabulary: adjectives

Match the adjectives with their opposites. There are two for each.

new	~~large~~	difficult	young	warm	rich
beautiful	~~big~~	hard	friendly	wealthy	pretty

1	small	*big*	*large*
2	old		
3	ugly		
4	easy		
5	poor		
6	cold		

Words from the story

Complete the sentences with words from the box.

> honeymoon injuries wedding was born separate jealous
> divorced ~~was born~~ buried funeral charities ill shy
> crowded pregnant married tunnel popular tours

1 Diana ....*was born*........ in July 1961.

2 Diana didn't like meeting lots of new people. She was very

....

3 In July 1981, Diana .... Prince Charles.

4 Many people wanted to see them after their .... in July 1981.

5 Two days later they went on .... on a big boat.

6 In October 1981, Diana got .... with her first baby.

7 In June 1982, Prince William ....

8 Soon after, Diana became very .... with eating problems.

9 Diana was very .... Lots of people loved her.

10 Diana began to work for .... to help people.

11 Camilla was often with Prince Charles, and Diana felt

....

12 In 1992, Charles and Diana decided not to live together – to

....

13 In 1996, Charles and Diana were .... They were not married any more.

14 Diana visited a lot of places and went on many .... of different countries.

15 In 1997, Diana and Dodi's car crashed in a .... in Paris.

16 Diana's .... were very serious and she died on 31st August.

17 Soon after, thousands of people went to London for Diana's
....

18 On this day, the streets were very .... – there were a
lot of people.

19 Diana was .... at her family home at Althorp.

Pronunciation: word stress

**Find the words with two or three syllables in the box on page 57. Then
put them into the correct stress pattern columns below. Three words are
done for you.**

◯ o	◯ o o	o ◯
married	*funeral*	*divorced*

Grammar: regular past simple

Complete the sentences with past simple forms of the verbs in the box.

arrive   ask   visit   wait   talk   save   want   work
~~move~~   invite   like   marry   start   divorce   love

1 Diana ..... *moved* ..... to London to live with friends.

2 Diana .... playing tennis and swimming.

3 Sometimes, the Spencer family .... the Royal Family at
their home.

4 Diana .... her father very much.

5 Diana's parents .... in 1969.

6 When Johnnie was very ill, his second wife .... his life.

7 Charles .... Diana to go on holiday with him.

8 Camilla .... Andrew Parker Bowles in 1973.

9 In 1981, Charles .... Diana to marry him.

10 Diana was very happy when she .... home with baby
William.

11 Diana's sisters .... for *Vogue* magazine.

12 Many people .... to Diana about their problems.

13 Diana .... to make a new life for herself and her sons.

14 Diana .... to help people with their problems.

15 Photographers .... outside the hotel for Diana and Dodi
to leave.

Sounds: regular past simple endings

**Put the past simple forms of the verbs above into the correct '-ed' sound
category. Three words are done for you.**

/ t /	/ d /	/ ɪd /
lik<u>ed</u>	arriv<u>ed</u>	wait<u>ed</u>

Grammar: irregular past simple

a   What are the past forms of these irregular verbs? The first one is done for you.

Infinitive	Past simple	Infinitive	Past simple
1 bring	*brought*	10 know	
2 come		11 leave	
3 eat		12 meet	
4 feel		13 read	
5 fly		14 speak	
6 find		15 spend	
7 give		16 take	
8 go		17 understand	
9 have		18 wear	

b   Use some of the past simple verbs above to complete the sentences. The first one is done for you.

1   Charles ...... *met* ...... Camilla for the first time at a polo match.

2   Diana often .... to her sister's house.

3   Diana .... happy after she married Charles.

4   Reporters .... lots of photographs of Diana.

5   Diana .... to Sarah about her problems.

6   James Hewitt listened to Diana and .... her problems.

7   Diana .... lots of time with Hasnat Khan.

8   Diana .... by plane to countries all over the world.

9   Diana .... beautiful clothes every day.

Grammar: past simple negatives

To make past simple <u>positive</u> sentences use:
subject + past simple + object
Charles   liked   hunting.

To make past simple <u>negative</u> sentences use:
subject + did not / didn't + infinitive + object
Diana   didn't   like   hunting.

Write these sentences in the negative form.

1   Diana liked Raine.

_____

2   Charles had many friends.

_____

3   Charles wanted to marry.

_____

4   Charles understood Diana.

_____

5   Diana had a private life.

_____

6   Diana wanted a divorce.

_____

7   The Royal Family came to London.

_____

8   Photographers took lots of pictures.

_____

Multiple choice

Choose the best answer. The first one is done for you.

1 When Diana's parents separated, she lived:
   a with her mother.
   b with her father. ✓
   c at boarding school.

2 In 1980, Prince Charles invited Diana:
   a to Buckingham Palace.
   b on a boat.
   c to a party.

3 Prince Charles liked:
   a being with Diana.
   b being with his family.
   c being with Camilla.

4 When Diana's book was first printed, people were:
   a happy.
   b afraid.
   c shocked.

5 Later, Diana started to help people with:
   a car crash injuries.
   b landmine injuries.
   c accident injuries.

6 Hasnat Khan didn't want to marry Diana because:
   a of his religion.
   b he loved his job.
   c he wanted to be famous.

7 When Diana met Dodi:
   a he was single.
   b he was married.
   c he had a girlfriend.

Diana's Charities

National AIDS Trust
New City Cloisters
196 Old Street
London
EC1V 9FR
Tel: 020 7814 6767
Fax: 020 7216 0111
Email: info@nat.org.uk
www.nat.org.uk

Help the Aged
207–221 Pentonville Road,
London
N1 9UZ
Tel: 020 7278 1114
Fax: 020 7278 1116
Email: info@helptheaged.org.uk
www.helptheaged.org.uk

Barnado's
Tanners Lane
Barkingside
Ilford
Essex
IG6 1QG
Tel: 020 8550 8822
Fax: 020 8551 6870
Email: dorothy.howes@barnardos.
  org.uk
www.barnardos.org.uk

**The Diana, Princess of Wales
Memorial Fund**
The County Hall
Westminster Bridge Road
London
SE1 7PB
Tel: 020 7902 5500
Fax: 020 7902 5511
Email: memorial.fund@memfund.
  org.uk
www.theworkcontinues.org

Centrepoint
Central House,
25 Camperdown Street
London
E1 8DZ
Tel: 0845 466 3400
Fax: 0845 466 3500
Email: info@centrepoint.org
www.centrepoint.org.uk

Sentebale
Clarence House
London
SW1A 1BA
Tel: 020 7024 5673
Fax: 020 7024 5660
Email: info@sentebale.org
www.sentebale.org/home/index.
html

**International Campaign to Ban
Landmines**
9 Rue de Cornavin
CH-1201 Geneva
Switzerland
Tel: 0229 200 325
Fax: 0229 200 115
E-mail: icbl@icbl.org
www.icbl.org

Published by Macmillan Heinemann ELT
Between Towns Road, Oxford OX4 3PP
A division of Macmillan Publishers Limited
Companies and representatives throughout the world
Heinemann is the registered trademark of Pearson Education, used under licence.

ISBN 978–0–2307–3116–5
ISBN 978–0–2307–1653–7 (with CD edition)

First published 2009
Text © Macmillan Publishers Limited 2009
Design and illustration © Macmillan Publishers Limited 2009
This version first published 2009

Cover photograph by Getty / Gemma Levine / Hulton Archive

The authors and publishers would like to thank the following for permission to
reproduce their photographic material:
Alamy/ Graham Harrison p17, Alamy/ Justin Leighton p51; Corbis/ Corbis/
Vanderlei Almeida/Reuters p26, Corbis/Mike Finn-Kelcey/Reuters p24,
Corbis/Reuters pp 33, 40; Getty Images p5, Getty Images/AFP p36, Getty
Images/ Tim Graham p9, Getty Images/ Popperfoto pp 7,10; Rex Features
pp 20, 45, 48.

Printed and bound in Thailand

Without CD edition

2014 2013 2012 2011 2010 2009
10   9   8   7   6   5   4   3   2   1

With CD edition

2014 2013 2012 2011 2010 2009
10   9   8   7   6   5   4   3   2   1